Student Response Book

Summer Success® Reading

James F. Baumann • Michael F. Opitz • Laura Robb

EDUCATION GROUP
A Houghton Mifflin Company

Credits

Writer: Priscilla Mullins

Design/Production: Jim Bartosik/Andy Cox, Ed Pokorski

Illustration: Chris Vallo and Jim Higgins

Poetry credits: "I Want You to Meet" by David McCord. From *One at a Time* by David McCord. Copyright © 1961, 1962 by David McCord. By permission of Little, Brown and Company (Inc.). "How a Puppy Grows" from *The Jolly Jungle Picture Book* by Leroy F. Jackson, copyright © 1926. "Maxie and the Taxi" by Dennis Lee. From *The Ice Cream Store* (originally published by HarperCollins Publishers Ltd., 1991). Copyright © 1991 Dennis Lee. With permission of the author. "Before the Monkey's Cage" from *Pickpocket Songs* by Edna Becker, copyright © 1935 by The Caxton Printers, Ltd. Caldwell, Idaho. "First Snow" by Marie Louise Allen. TEXT COPYRIGHT © 1957 BY MARIE ALLEN HOWARTH. Used by permission of HarperCollins Publishers.

Copyright © 2001 by Great Source Education Group, a division of Houghton Mifflin Company. All rights reserved.

Permission is hereby granted to teachers to reprint or photocopy in classroom quantities the pages or sheets in this work that carry a copyright notice, provided each copy made shows the copyright notice. Such copies may not be sold, and further distribution is expressly prohibited. Except as authorized above, prior written permission must be obtained from Great Source Education Group to reproduce or transmit this work or portions thereof in any other form or by any other electronic or mechanical means, including any information storage or retrieval system, unless expressly permitted by federal copyright law. Address inquiries to Great Source Education Group, 181 Ballardvale Street, Wilmington, Massachusetts 01887.

Great Source® is a registered trademark of Houghton Mifflin Company.

Summer Success™ is a trademark of Houghton Mifflin Company.

Printed in the United States of America

International Standard Book Number: 0-669-48522-5

4 5 6 7 8 9 10 - MZ - 07 06 05

Name _____ Date _____

Questions Good Readers Ask Themselves

Connect It
- What do I know about . . . ?
- What does this make me think of?

Picture It
- What picture do I see in my mind?

Understand It
- Does it make sense?
- If I don't understand something, what can I do?

Question It
- What is the most important idea?
- What questions do I have?

Wrap It Up
- What happened in this story?

Name _____ Date _____

Reading Log

Draw and write about each book you read.

Name _____ Date _____

Summer Success: Reading 5

Name _____ Date _____

Things Good Readers Do to Read Words

Look at the whole word
- Look at the beginning of the word.
- Look at the middle of the word.
- Look at the end of the word.

Look at parts of the word
- Look for parts of the word that you know.

Look at the whole page
- Think what would make sense.
- Look at the pictures.

Name _____ Date _____

Word Bank

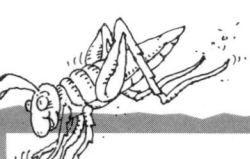

Week 1
_____
_____
_____
_____

Week 2
_____
_____
_____
_____

Week 3
_____
_____
_____
_____

Week 4
_____
_____
_____
_____

Week 5
_____
_____
_____
_____

Week 6
_____
_____
_____
_____

Name _____ Date _____

ABC's
abcd efg hijk lmnop
qrs tuv wx yz

Aa apple

Bb butterfly

Cc cat

Dd dog

Ee elephant

Ff fish

Gg guitar

Hh helicopter

Ii igloo

Jj jar

Kk kangaroo

Ll lion

Mm moon

Nn nest

Oo octopus

Pp pig

Qq quilt

Rr rhinoceros

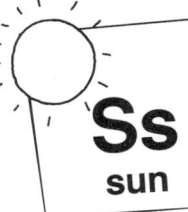
Ss sun

Tt turtle

Uu umbrella

Vv vacuum cleaner

Ww watermelon

Xx xylophone

Yy yo-yo

Zz zebra

Summer Success: Reading

Summer Success: Reading

Dear Parent or Caregiver,

This summer, your child will be using the **Summer Success: Reading** program. This program will provide instruction in reading skills and strategies to help your child read better. **Summer Success: Reading** features different types of reading (fiction, nonfiction, poetry) and topics. Each week, your child will bring home a weekly newsletter so you will be able to keep in touch with your child's activities in summer school.

Summer Success: Reading emphasizes reading strategies. This means that the program has instruction in helping your child understand what he or she is reading. One example of a strategy is "making connections." A reader who makes connections asks questions like "What do I know about this?" "What does this remind me of?" "How am I like this character?" When a reader can make connections, she or he understands the text.

Summer Success: Reading also works with words, helping your child become better at reading and writing words. A section of the lesson called Read & Explore Words focuses on how words work. Children will study words, make words from letters, classify words, and—in general—get to know words.

But we cannot do it alone at school. We need your help as well. On the back of this letter are things you can do at home to support the summer school program. Doing reading and writing activities every day will help your child develop her or his reading ability this summer and beyond. Please let me know if you have any questions. Thank you.

Educationally yours,

Your child's teacher

Summer Success: Reading

Name _____ Date _____

Read, Read, Read!

The more you read with your child, the more opportunities he or she will have to enjoy reading and improve reading skills. Try to have a variety of books at home. If you don't know what books to get, ask other children what they like to read. Librarians, bookstore workers, and teachers are good resources, too.

Make sure your child reads every day.

- Read aloud to your child.
- Take turns with your child reading paragraphs or pages.
- As you read together, ask your child what he or she thinks. Share your thoughts, too.

Model how to think about the text. Say things like,

"This reminds me of —"

"I wonder why —"

"I predict that —"

"I would like to ask the author—"

When your child has free time, try one of these ideas.

- Read a book.
- Read a magazine or newspaper.
- Read a recipe and cook something.
- Make up a play with a friend.
- Write your own story.

Week 1

Name _____ Date _____

I Want You to Meet . . .

by David McCord

. . . Meet Ladybug,

her little sister Sadiebug,

her mother, Mrs. Gradybug,

her aunt, that nice oldmaidybug,

and Baby—she's a fraidybug.

Draw a picture of Ladybug. Write about your picture.

My Ladybug has spots an his bach it has wings under its wings cuvrh.

Summer Success: Reading 13

Week 1

Name _____ Date _____

A Bug I Like

Draw a bug you like. Write about your bug.

Bugs loves fnot it
glrings the jous in
it.

Week 1

Name _____ Date _____

Word Parts

Say each picture name.

Tell how many word parts each picture name has.
Write 1, 2, or 3.

spider   **pencil**   **computer**

2   2   3

butterfly   **frog**   **cup**

3   1   1

Summer Success: Reading

Week 1

Name _____ Date _____

Sara's Garden

Write what you saw in Sara's garden.

ants

a spider

bees

a frog

1 I saw ants _____

2 I saw a spider _____

3 I saw bees _____

4 I saw a frog _____

Week 1

Name _____ Date _____

In Sara's Garden

Write a new sentence about Sara's garden.

Draw a picture.

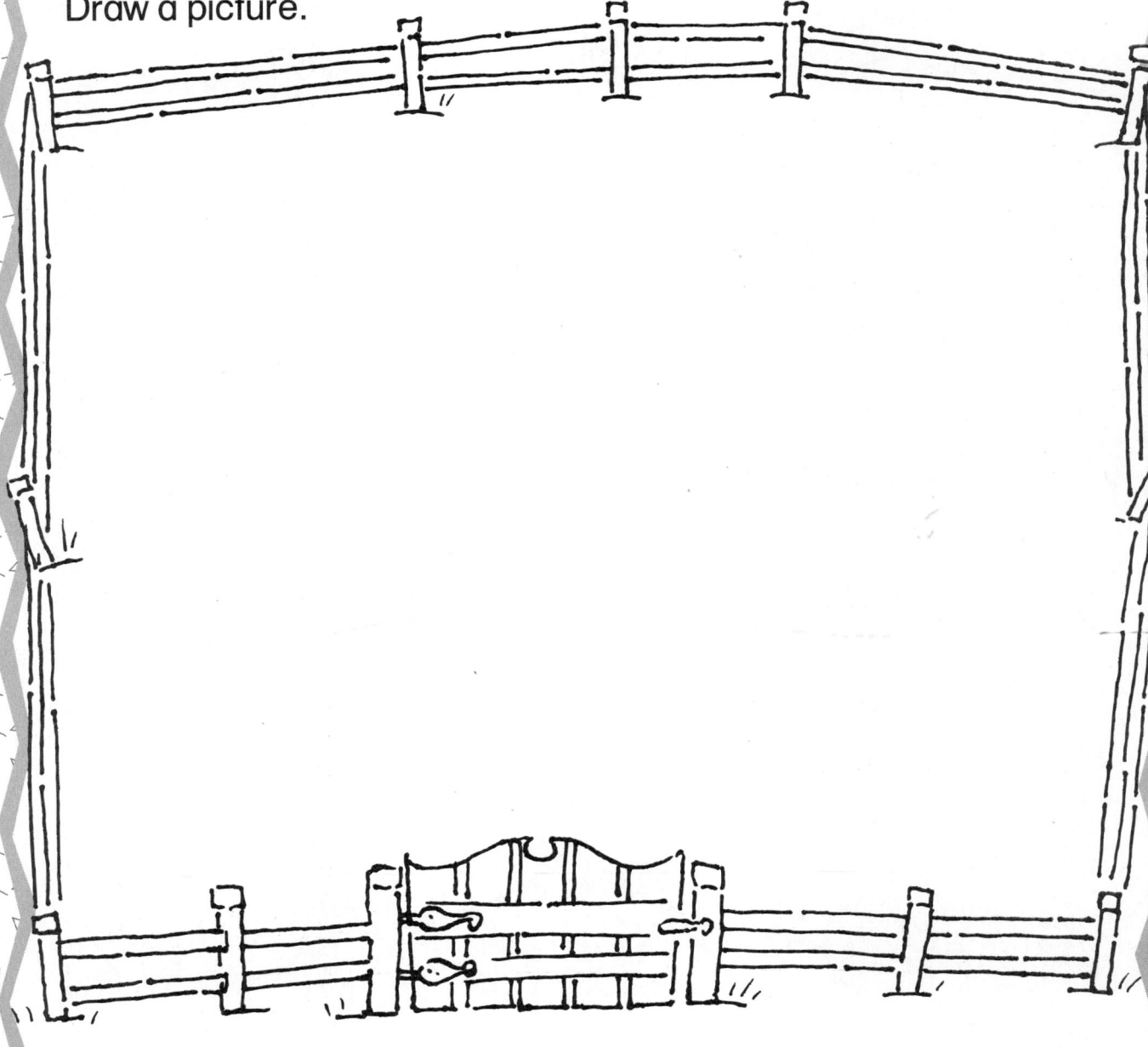

_____ in Sara's garden.

Summer Success: Reading

Week 1

Name _____ Date _____

Make Words

Write **an** words and **at** words.

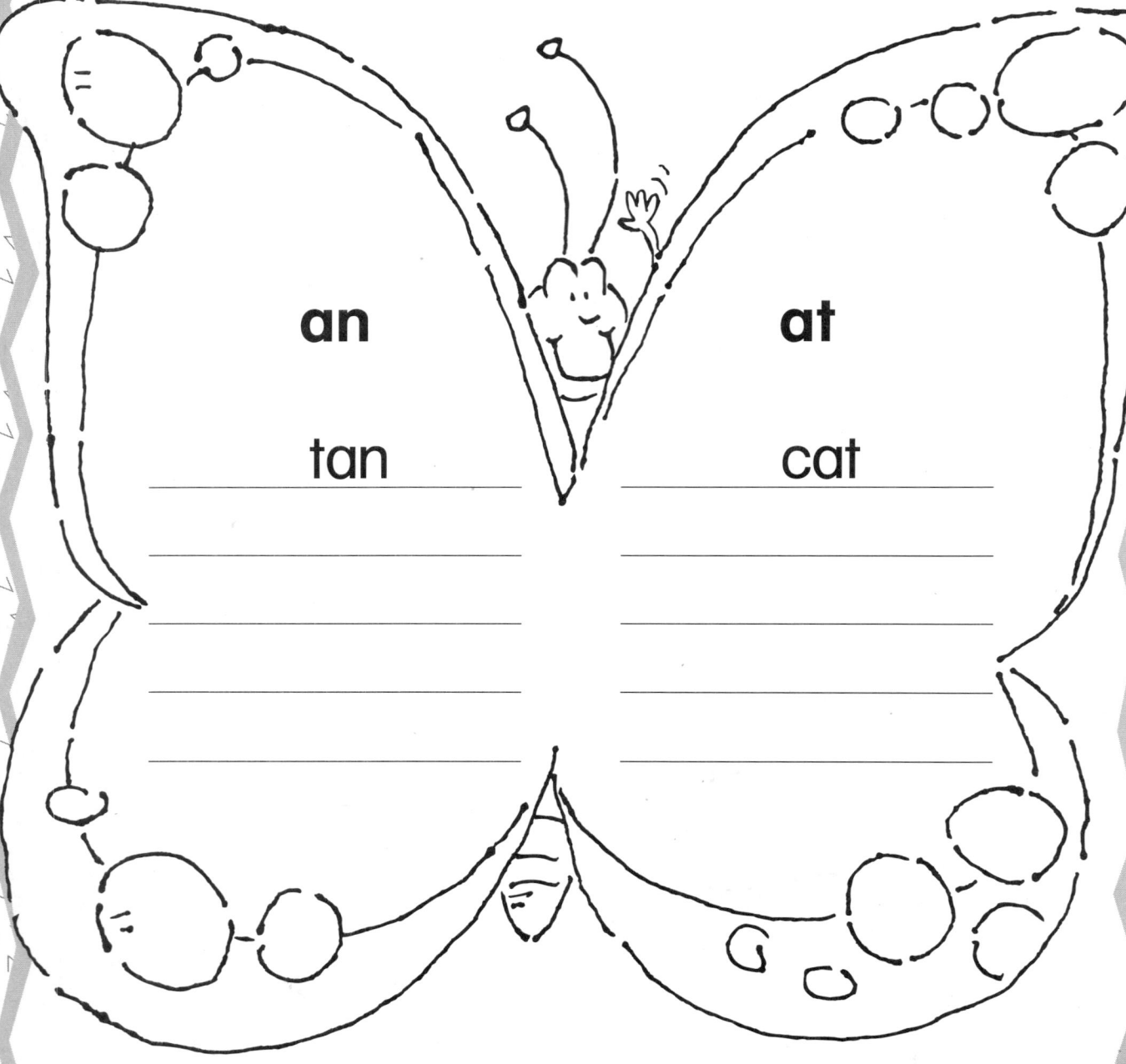

an

tan

at

cat

18 Summer Success: Reading

Week 1

Name _____ Date _____

Find the Bug

Find the name of each bug.

Write the name of each bug the right way.

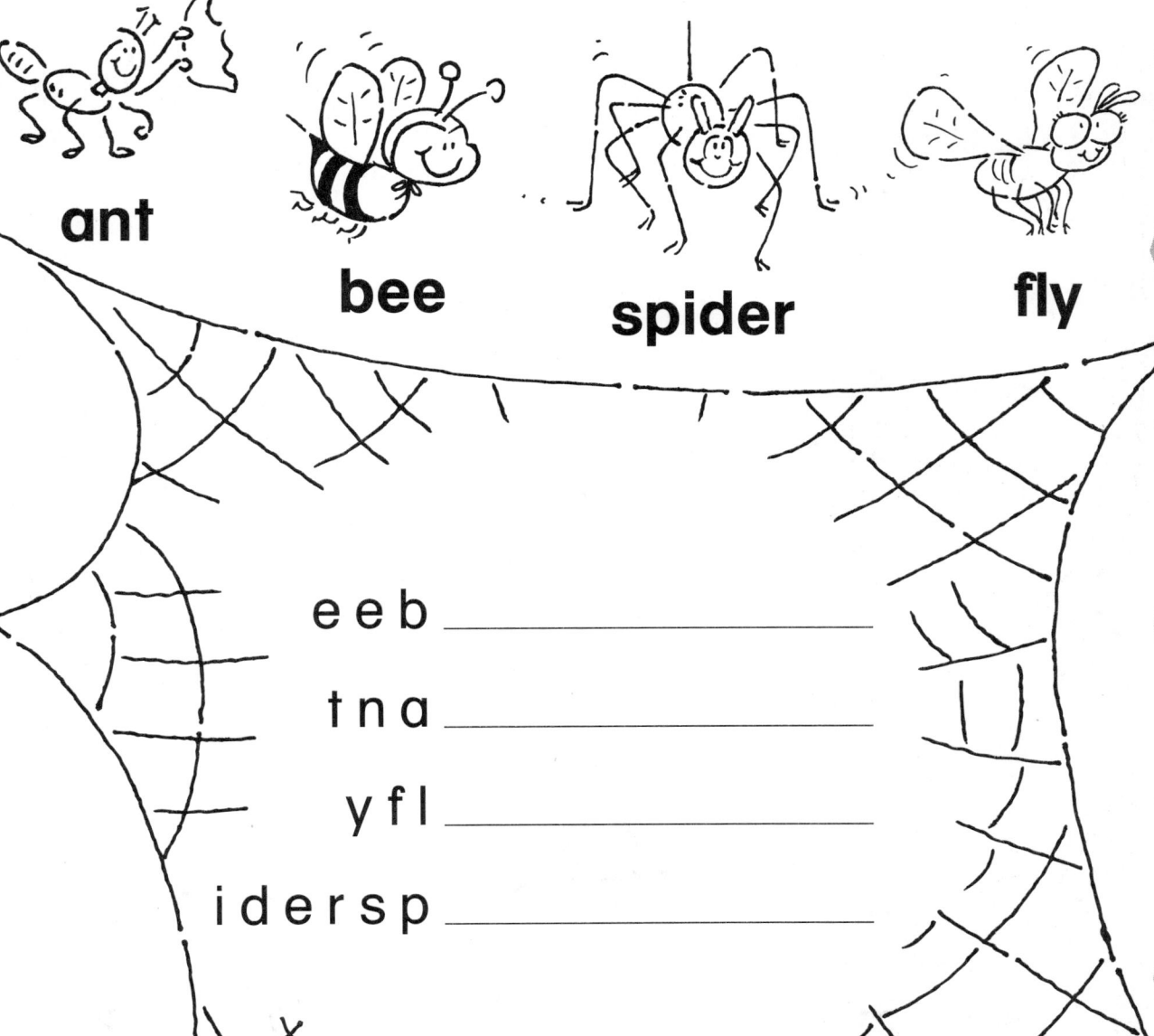

ant   bee   spider   fly

e e b _____

t n a _____

y f l _____

i d e r s p _____

Summer Success: Reading 19

Week 1

Name _____ Date _____

The Beginning Sound

Circle the words that begin with **b**.

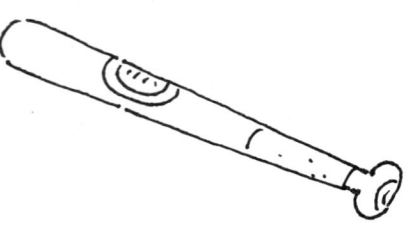  

Summer Success: Reading

Week 1

Name _____ Date _____

I Love Bugs!

Draw the bugs you love.

Write what you love about bugs.

I love _____

_____

Summer Success: Reading 21

Week 1

Name _____ Date _____

Self-Evaluation

1 Two words I learned this week are
_____
_____

2 The best story I read this week was _____
_____
_____

3 Next week I will try to _____
_____
_____
_____
_____

Fold along gray line.

Take It Home!

BUG PARTY

How many words can you find that start with the letter <u>b</u>?

12   1

Then the bugs ate some baked beans.

They asked all the bugs to come.

10   3

Some bugs picked berries in the bushes.

All the bugs played baseball.

8   5

Summer Success: Reading   23

Fold along gray line.

The bees had a party on the beach.

2

And they ate all the berries from the bowl.

11

The bugs brought bats and balls.

4

They put the berries in a big bowl.

9

The bugs blew big balloons.

6

The bugs bounced their beach balls.

7

Week 1 Newsletter

This week we read about bugs. We read the book *A Firefly Named Torchy* and a magazine called *Bugs*. We also read two poems and a nonfiction story about walking sticks, moths, and cabbage worms. Ask your child what he or she learned from reading and thinking about these stories.

The word of the week was *ants*. Students played word games using this word. They also made up new words from the letters in *ants,* such as *an* and *sat*.

Here is what your child has to say, in words and in pictures, about the week:

_____
_____
_____
_____

Summer Success: Reading

Week 1 Newsletter

Reading at Home

One way to help your child become a better reader is to read to him or her every day. As children listen to stories, they develop the skills they need to become independent readers.

Here are some books about bugs that you and your child may enjoy reading together.

***About Insects* by Cathryn Sill (Peachtree, 2000)** This book is an introduction to the anatomy, behavior, and habitat of various insects, including the beetle, moth, and cockroach. The illustrations are realistic with good detail.

***Bugs!* by Patricia and Fredrick McKissack (Children's Press, 2000)** Simple, patterned text and illustrations of a variety of insects introduce the numbers one through five.

***Bugs, Beetles, and Butterflies* by Harriet Ziefert (Puffin, 1998)** Simple, rhyming text introduces many different kinds of bugs, including beetles, earwigs, and butterflies.

***Bugs! Bugs! Bugs!* by Bob Barner (Chronicle, 1999)** This book of silly rhymes includes a chart with amusing facts about each bug featured in the text.

***Buzz, Buzz, Buzz* by Byron Barton (Aladdin, 1995)** A buzzing bee bites the rump of a bull, setting off a hilarious chain reaction.

***A Flea Story* by Leo Lionni (Knopf, 1995)** Two fleas have a conversation while riding on the backs of different animals.

***In the Tall, Tall Grass* by Denise Fleming (Holt, 1995)** Rhyming text and colorful illustrations describe the movements of small grassland creatures and the sounds they make.

***Spider on the Floor* by Raffi (Crown, 1996)** In this illustrated song, a mischievous spider climbs all over an elderly woman and spins a web around her and a cast of other characters. Sheet music is included.

How a Puppy Grows

by Leroy F. Jackson

I think it's very funny
The way a puppy grows—
A little on his wiggle-tail,
A little on his nose,
A little on his tummy
And a little on his ears;
I guess he'll be a dog all
   right
In half a dozen years.

Draw a picture of the puppy in the poem.

Week 2

Name _____ Date _____

My Pet

Draw a picture of a pet you have or would like to have. Show where your pet lives and what it likes to eat. Write about your pet.

_____

_____

_____

Week 2

Name _____ Date _____

One or Two?

Clap the word parts you hear for each picture. If you hear one part, clap one time, and write 1 on the line. If you hear two parts, clap two times, and write 2 on the line.

1 _____   _____   _____

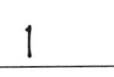  

_____   _____   _____

_____   _____   _____

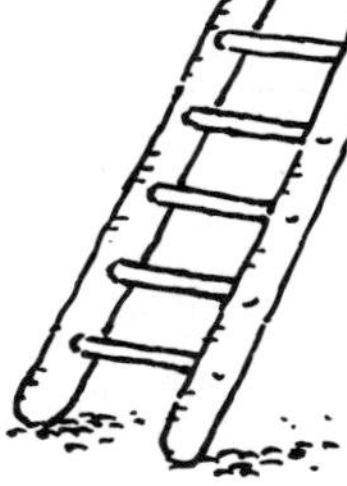

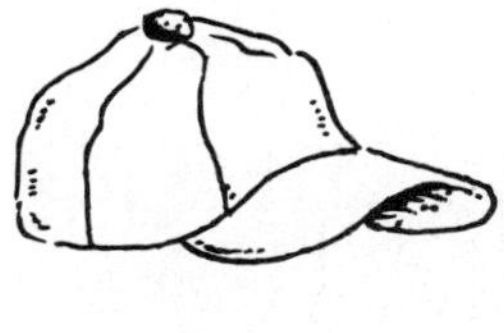

Name ______________________________ Date ______________

Whose Pet?

Draw a line from each pet to its owner.

1.
Kim

2.
Jim

3.
Ling

4.
Nick

5.
Tim

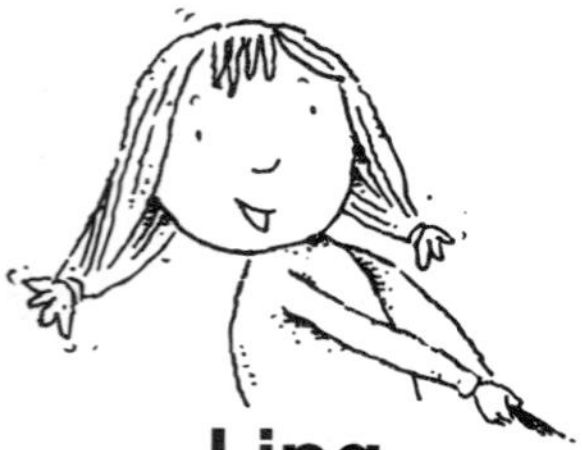

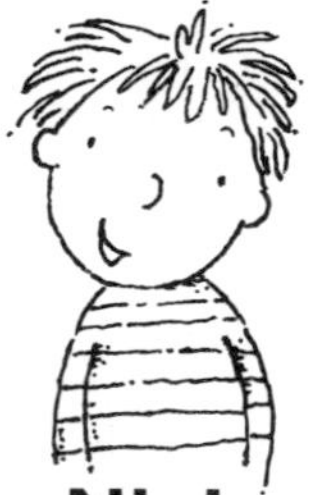

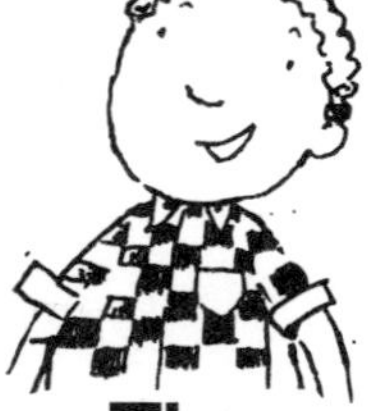

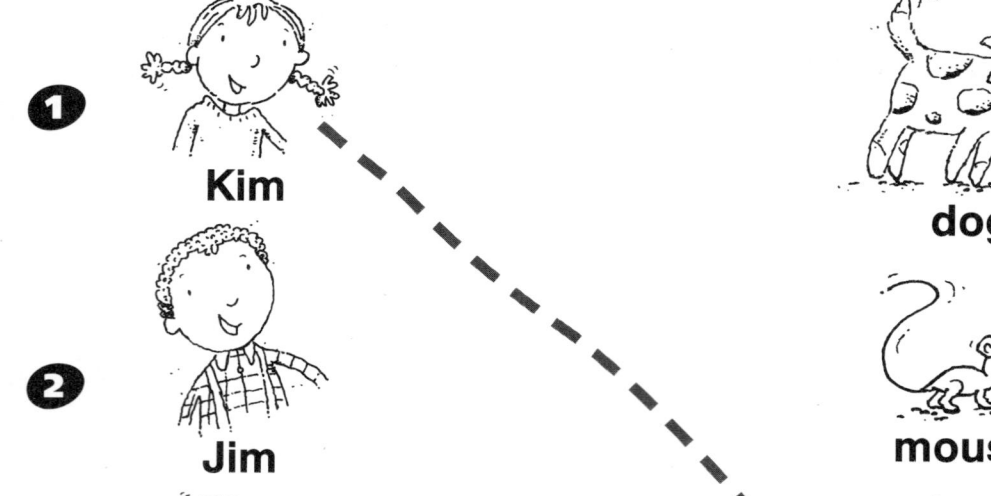

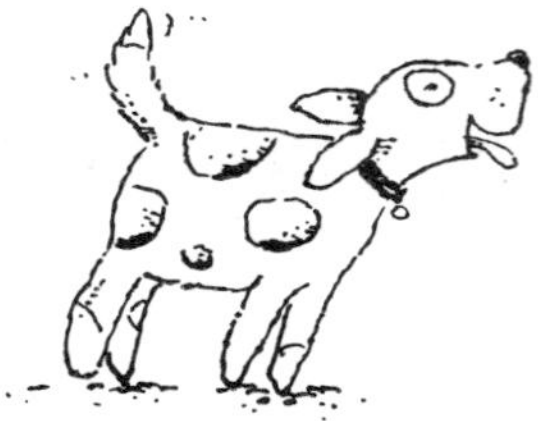

dog

mouse

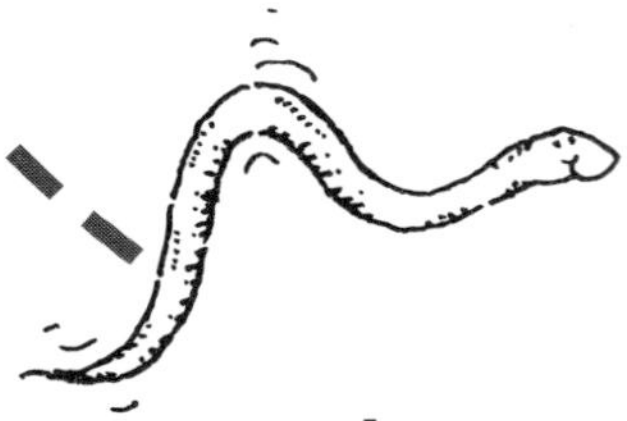

snake

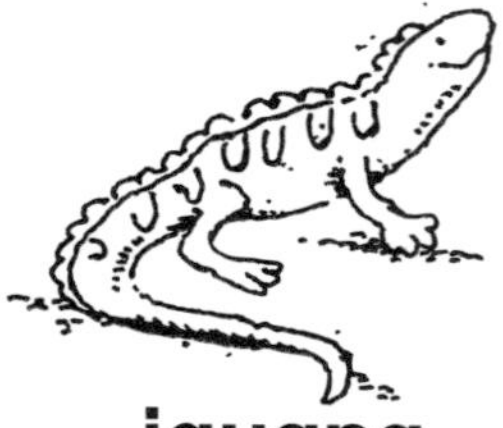

iguana

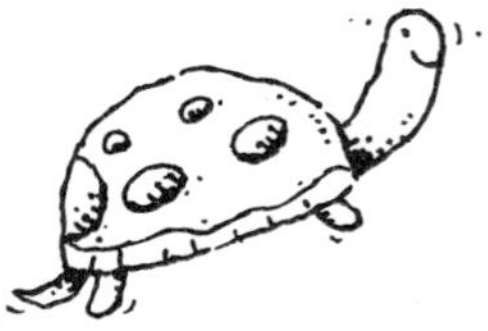

turtle

Week 2

Name _____ Date _____

Pet Show

Write and draw about a pet.

"This is my _____," says _____.

"It lives _____."

Week 2

Name _____ Date _____

Sam at School

Draw a picture of what Sam <u>could</u> do at the end of the story. Write about your picture.

"Sam <u>could</u> . . ."

_____

_____

Week 2

Name _____ Date _____

Sort by Syllable

Find the picture cards whose names have one syllable. Mix up all the cards again and find the picture cards whose names have two syllables. Then mix up all the cards again and find the picture cards whose names have three syllables.

 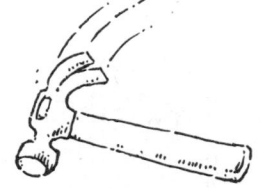

Summer Success: Reading 33

Name ______________________________ Date ____________

Rhymes with Cat

Look at the pictures and read the words below. Color the pictures that rhyme with cat. Put a big ✘ on the pictures that do not rhyme with cat.

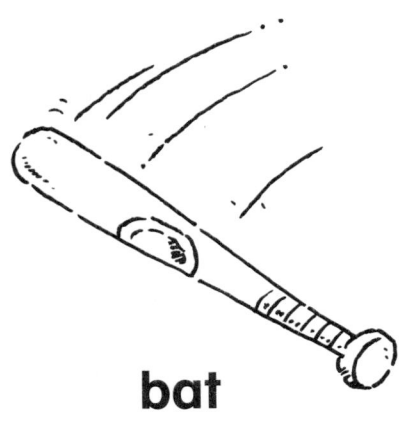

bat

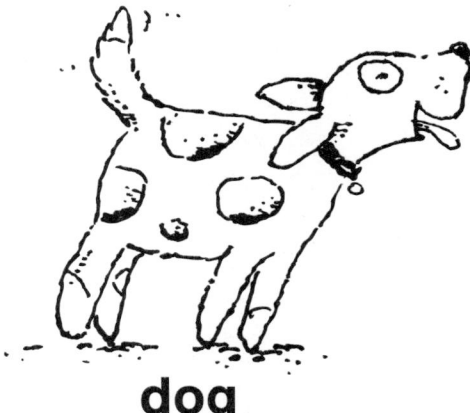

dog

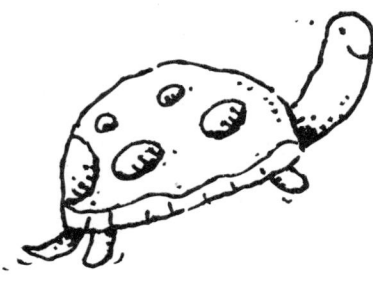

turtle

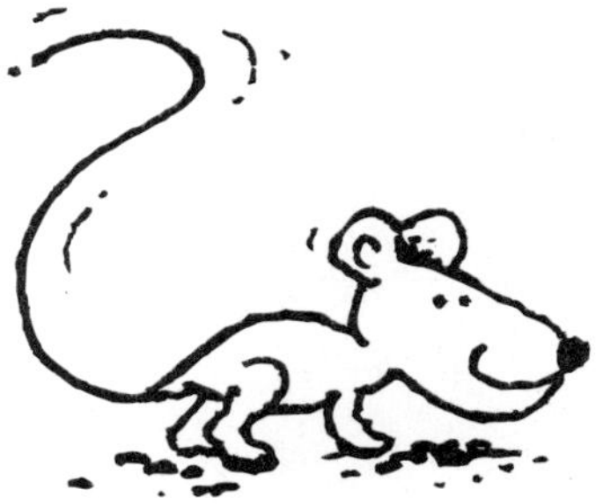

rat

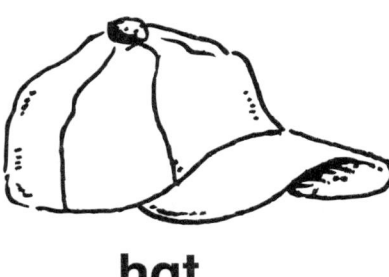

hat

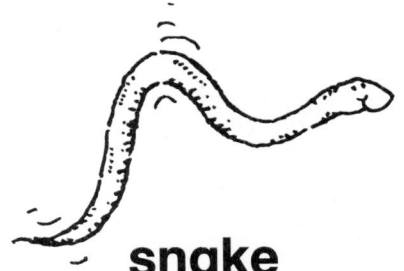

snake

Week 2

Name _____ Date _____

Self-Evaluation

1 Two words I learned this week are _____
_____
_____

2 The best story I read this week was _____
_____
_____

3 Next week I will try to _____
_____
_____

Take It Home!

Color the pets. Cut along the dashed lines. Mix the pieces up. Put the puzzle pieces back together to match each pet with the correct word.

dog

turtle

cat

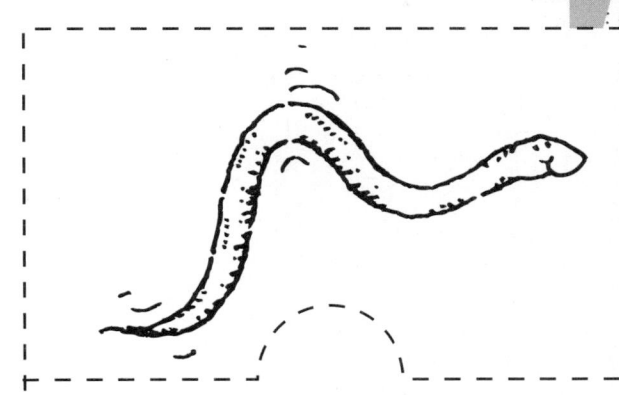

snake

Week 2 Newsletter

This week we read about pets. We read the book *Martha Blah Blah,* a magazine called *Pets,* and a poem about how dogs grow. We also read a funny story about a dog named Sam. Ask your child what he or she learned from reading and thinking about these stories.

The word of the week was *cats.* Children played word games using this word. They made words from the letters in *cats.* They also thought of words that rhyme with *cats.*

Here is what your child has to say, in words and in pictures, about the week:

_____
_____
_____
_____

Week 2 Newsletter

Pet Rhyme Time at Home

This week we learned some pet words and we did some rhyming. Read all of the words below to your child. First have your child listen for the rhyming words. Then have your child look at the page. Name each picture together. Have your child draw lines to match the rhyming words.

1. dog — cake
2. cat — bat
3. snake — log
4. fish — house
5. mouse — dish

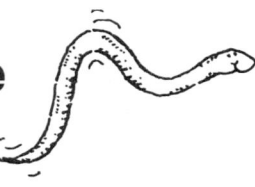

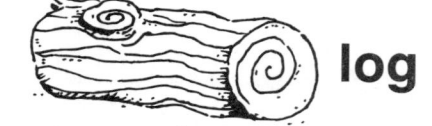

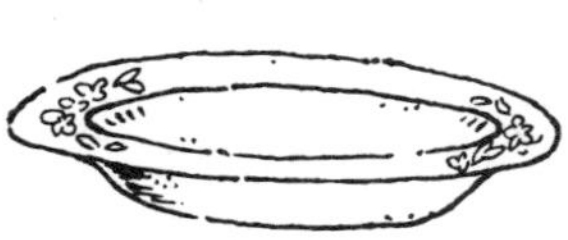

40 Summer Success: Reading

Maxie and the Taxi

by Dennis Lee

Maxie drove a taxi
With a *beep! beep! beep!*

And he picked up all the people
In a heap, heap, heap.

He took them to the farm
To see the sheep, sheep, sheep—

Then, Maxie and the taxi
Went to sleep, sleep, sleep.

Draw the taxi. Show one place it went. Write about your picture.

_____

_____

Week 3

Name _____ Date _____

Things on the Go

Think of ways people get from one place to another. Draw some of them here. Write about your pictures.

Week 3 Name _____ Date _____

Rhymes with Boats

Circle the pictures that rhyme with <u>boats</u>. Then write about boats.

boats

_____
_____
_____

Summer Success: Reading 43

Week 3

Name _____ Date _____

Picnic

Draw a picture of one part of the story. Write about your picture.

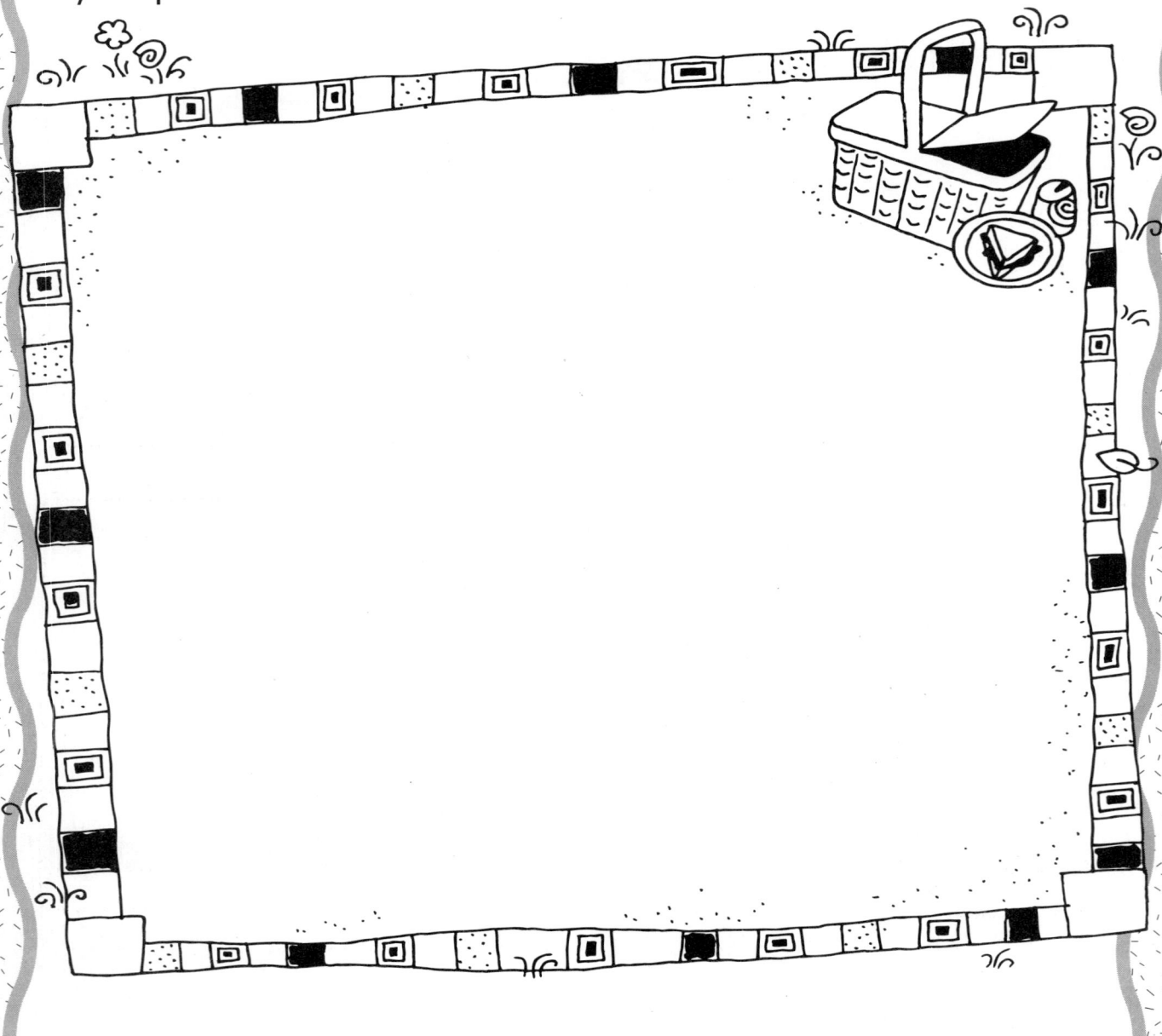

_____
_____

44 Summer Success: Reading

Week 3

Name _____ Date _____

Trucks I Know

Draw two different kinds of trucks. Write about your trucks.

Summer Success: Reading 45

Week 3

Name _____ Date _____

Float Your Boat

Name each picture below. Look on the boat to find the missing letters for each word. Write the missing letters on the lines.

b g c fl

1.  ____ o a t

2.  ____ o a t

3.  ____ o a t

4.  ____ o a t

46 Summer Success: Reading

Week 3

Name _____ Date _____

Trucks

Write your own sentences about trucks. Draw a picture for each sentence.

Trucks carry _____

Trucks carry _____

Week 3

Name _____ Date _____

Boat Word-Find Puzzle

Circle the word <u>boats</u> in the puzzle.

b o a t s x b
o b o a t s a
v p b o a t s
s b o a t s t
b o a t s v s

48 Summer Success: Reading

Week 3

Name _____ Date _____

Round and Round

Bus wheels are round. Think of other things that are round and draw them in the circles below. Label your pictures.

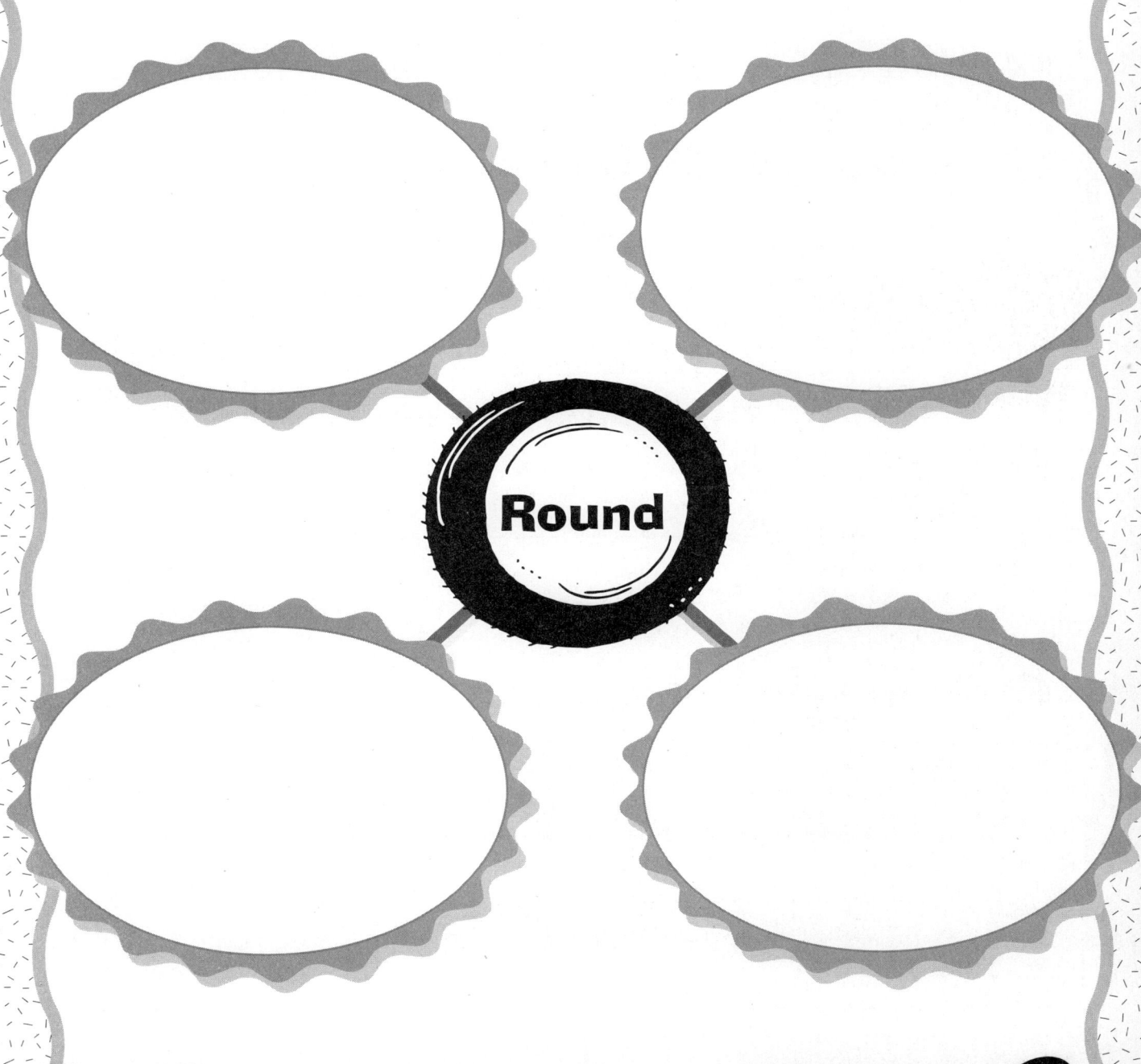

Round

Summer Success: Reading   49

Week 3

Name _____ Date _____

Self-Evaluation

1 Two words I learned this week are

_____

_____

2 Two ways to travel that I read about are _____

_____

_____

_____

3 The best story I read this week was _____

_____

_____

_____

4 Next week I will try to _____

_____

_____

_____

Summer Success: Reading

Cut along dashed lines.

Take It Home!

Cut along the dashed lines. Mix up the cards and turn them over. Play a memory matching game by finding the cards that are the same.

bike	bike
car	car
boat	boat
truck	truck
plane	plane

Summer Success: Reading 51

Week 3 Newsletter

This week we read about things that are "on the go." We read the book *This Is the Way We Go to School* and a magazine called *On the Go*. We also read a poem about transportation. Ask your child what he or she learned after reading and thinking about these stories.

The word of the week was *boats*. Children played word games using this word. They made up new words from the letters in *boats*. They thought of words that rhyme with *boats* and completed a word-find puzzle.

Here is what your child has to say, in words and in pictures, about the week:

_____
_____
_____
_____

Summer Success: Reading

Week 3 Newsletter

Letters on the Go at Home

Name each picture below with your child. Help your child choose the letter that is missing to complete each word. Have your child say the word and listen for the sound at the beginning.

t b
s
c p
h

1. _____ o a t

2. _____ r u c k

3. _____ l a n e

4. _____ a r

5. _____ k a t e s

6. _____ e l i c o p t e r

54 Summer Success: Reading

Week 4

Name _____ Date _____

At Grandpa's Farm

by Anonymous

I went out to my grandpa's farm.
The billy goat filled me with alarm.

He chased me up an apple tree,
And clinging there I still would be,

If grandpa hadn't come that day
And chased the billy goat away.

Draw what you would do if you saw a goat. Write about your picture.

Week 4 Name _____ Date _____

On the Farm

If you were a farmer, would you rather have an animal farm or a wheat farm? Draw your farm below. Tell why you drew this picture.

My Farm

Week 4

Name _____ Date _____

Who Feeds the Animals?

Under Will's picture, write the animal names that he fed.
Under Jill's picture, write the animal names that she fed.

Will   **Jill**

goats

horses

chickens

pigs

Summer Success: Reading

Week 4 Name _____ Date _____

Making Bread

Draw a picture to show how the wheat from a farm becomes bread for your table. Write about your picture.

Week 4

Name _____ Date _____

How Many Sounds?

Cut out the cards. Say the name of each picture slowly. Count the sounds. Write on the card the number of sounds you hear.

bee	cat	rug	house
key	bag	bell	hat

Summer Success: Reading

Week 4 Name _____ Date _____

Farm Animals

Draw two animals. Write what your animals are doing.

Week 4

Name _____ Date _____

Find the Word Farms

The word farms is in the puzzle 5 times. Look for the word farms. Circle it.

f	a	r	m	s	n	k
b	c	f	a	r	m	s
t	f	a	r	m	s	u
f	a	r	m	s	f	a
d	f	a	r	m	s	r

Farm Words

Draw a picture to show what scared the little boy away from the barn. Write about your picture.

There Was a Little Boy

There was a little boy went into a barn,
And lay down on some hay;
An owl came out and flew about,
And the little boy ran away.

Week 4 Name _____ Date _____

Self-Evaluation

1 Two words I learned this week are _____

_____

_____

2 The best story I read this week was _____

_____

3 I liked the story because _____

_____

4 Next week I will try to _____

_____

_____

Fold along gray line.

Take It Home!

That is what the animals say!

What Do the Animals Say?

8

1

What do cows say?

Pigs say, "Oink!"

6

3

Summer Success: Reading **65**

Fold along gray line.

What do pigs say?

Cows say, "Moo!"

Moo Moo Moo

2

7

What do horses say?

Horses say, "Neigh!"

Neigh Neigh

4

5

Cut along dashed lines.

© Great Source. Permission is granted to copy this page.

66 Summer Success: Reading

Week 4 Newsletter

This week we read about things that are on farms. We read the book *One Fine Day* and a magazine called *On the Farm*. We also read a poem about farms. Ask your child what he or she learned from reading and thinking about these stories.

The word of the week was *farms*. The class played word games using this word. They made words with the letters in *farms*. They also completed a word-find puzzle looking for the word *farms*.

Here is what your child has to say, in words and in pictures, about the week:

_____
_____
_____
_____

Summer Success: Reading

Week 4 Newsletter

You and Your Child

One of the best things you can do with your child is read! Set aside time each day to read with your child. Many families find that reading a story or two (or three!) at bedtime serves as a regular routine to help children wind down at the end of the day.

Any books will do, but here are some titles that you might find at the library or bookstore. The books listed below are all about farms and farm animals.

***Chicken Little* retold by Laura Rader (HarperCollins, 1998)**
A retelling of the traditional story about a little chick who thinks the sky is falling because an acorn has fallen on her head.

***The Farm* by Isidro Sanchez (Barron's, 1991)**
A brother and sister go to their grandparents' farm for vacation. There they learn how vegetables are grown and shipped to market.

***The Little Red Hen* by Byron Barton (HarperCollins, 1997)**
A little red hen plants wheat, grinds flour, and bakes bread all by herself, but all the other farm animals want to help her eat it.

***The Quiet Little Farm* by Janet Kerr (Holt, 2000)**
Once there was a quiet little farm with snow all around. As winter turned to spring, the baby farm animals came out to play. With all the ruckus they made, the quiet little farm wasn't quiet anymore.

***Spots, Feathers, and Curly Tails* by Nancy Tafuri (Morrow, 1991)**
A series of questions and answers about the characteristics of different farm animals.

Week 5

Name _____ Date _____

Before the Monkey's Cage

by Edna Becker

The monkey curled his tail about—
 It looked like so much fun
That as I stood and watched him there,
 I wished that I had one.

Draw a picture that shows where you would keep a monkey if you could have one. Write about your picture.

Summer Success: Reading

Week 5 Name _____ Date _____

Zoo Animal Names

Write the name of each animal that came to Leslie's house.

1. _____

2. _____

3. _____

4. _____

5. _____

Week 5

Name _____ Date _____

The Zoo at Leslie's House

Draw what you "see" when you picture the animals at Leslie's house. Write about your drawing.

My Picture

My Words

Summer Success: Reading 71

Week 5 Name _____ Date _____

What Did You See?

Draw and write what the boys in the story saw, did, and learned.

Week 5

Name _____ Date _____

Tigers

Write the words you can make from the word <u>tigers</u>. Write one word in each box.

t i g e r s

Week 5

Name _____ Date _____

What Did You See at the Zoo?

Write what you saw at the zoo.
Draw a picture.

What did you see at the zoo?

I saw _____, _____,

_____, and _____.

That's what I saw at the zoo.

Week 5

Name _____ Date _____

Begins the Same

Cut out the picture box of the tiger and the lion. Then cut out the picture cards. Put them under the picture whose name begins with the same sound.

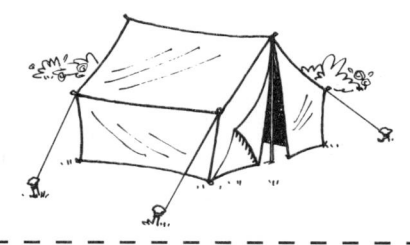

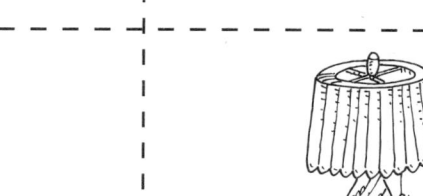

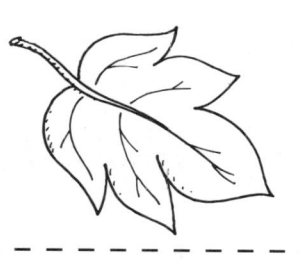

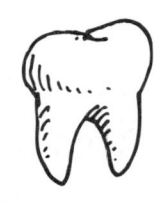

tiger | lion

Summer Success: Reading 75

Week 5

Name _____ Date _____

Insect Zoo

What insect would you like to see at an insect zoo? Draw the insect. Write why you want to see that insect.

Summer Success: Reading 77

Week 5

Name _____ Date _____

Self-Evaluation

1 Two words I learned this week are
_____
_____

2 The best story I read this week was _____
_____
_____
_____

3 I liked the story because _____
_____
_____
_____

4 Next week I will try to _____
_____
_____
_____

Fold along gray line.

Take It Home!

The monkeys see me!

Do You See the Animals?

8

1

Do you see the lions?

Do you see the giraffes?

6

3

Cut along dashed lines.

© Great Source. Permission is granted to copy this page.

Summer Success: Reading 79

Fold along gray line.

Do you see the zebras?

Do you see the monkeys?

2

7

Do you see the hippos?

Do you see the llamas?

4

5

Cut along dashed lines.

© Great Source. Permission is granted to copy this page.

80 Summer Success: Reading

Week 5 Newsletter

This week we read about an animal zoo and an insect zoo. We read the book *If Anything Ever Goes Wrong at the Zoo* and a magazine called *At the Zoo*. We also read two poems about zoos. Ask your child what he or she learned from reading and thinking about these stories.

The word of the week was *tigers*. Students played word games using this word. They made up new words from the letters in *tigers*.

Here is what your child has to say, in words and in pictures, about the week:

_____

_____

_____

_____

Summer Success: Reading

Week 5 Newsletter

You and Your Child

You can create simple games at home that will help your child be more aware of letters and the sounds that letters stand for.

- As you are riding in the car or walking down the street, look for the letters of the alphabet. (S on a stop sign, T on a theater, U on a U-turn sign)

- Look in the weekly grocery store circular to find foods that start with the same sound. ("Let's find something that begins like pull. Here are popcorn, pears, and pocket bread.")

- Play I'm Thinking. Give your child clues for the word you are thinking of. ("I'm thinking of an animal. It is black and white and starts with /z/*.")

- Point out words when you read to your child. ("Here's a word that starts just like your name, Kara. This is the word kite.")

★ A letter between two slashes means that you should say the sound associated with the letter, not the letter name.

First Snow

by Marie Louise Allen

Snow makes whiteness where it falls.

The bushes look like popcorn-balls.

The places where I always play

Look like somewhere else today.

Draw the bushes in the snow.

Week 6

Name _____ Date _____

The Weather Today

Draw the weather today.

Write about the weather.

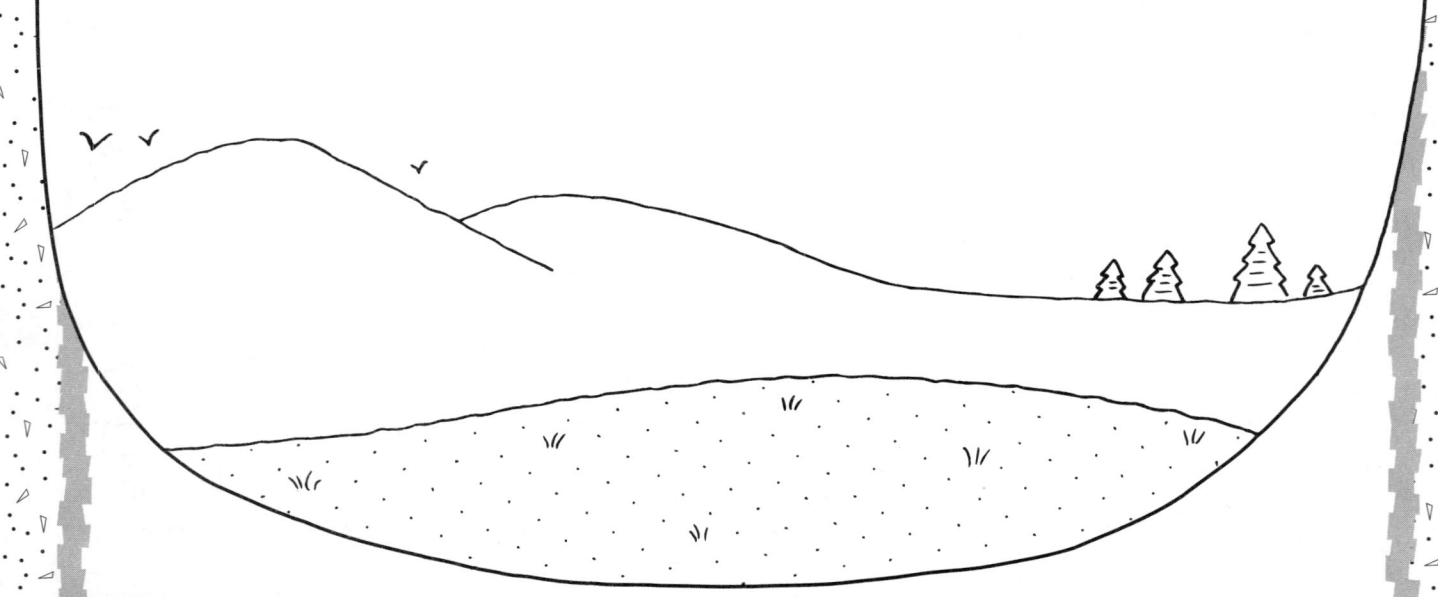

Week 6

Name _____ Date _____

The Sounds of Weather

How does each sound word begin?

Choose the letter or letters from each box.

Write the letter or letters on the line.

1 rain _____ums   p dr wh

2 hail _____ings   cr gr p

3 wind _____istles   wh dr cr

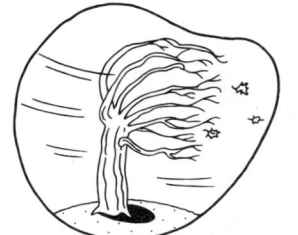

4 lightning _____acks   gr cr dr

5 thunder _____owls   wh dr gr

Summer Success: Reading

Week 6

Name _____ Date _____

Weather Sayings

Pick a saying from "When It Rains."

Write the saying you like best. Draw a picture of the saying.

__Week 6__

Name _____ Date _____

Word Fun

Write the words in the correct group.

| snow | on | now | won | son | so | no |

2 letters

_____
_____
_____

3 letters

_____
_____
_____

4 letters

_____

Summer Success: Reading 87

Week 6

Name _____ Date _____

Stormy Weather

Say the name of each storm.

Color the pictures that begin with the same sound or sounds.

hurricane

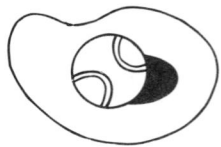

tornado

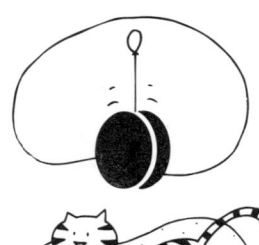

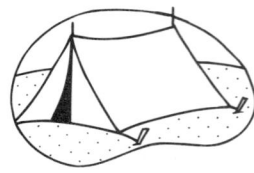

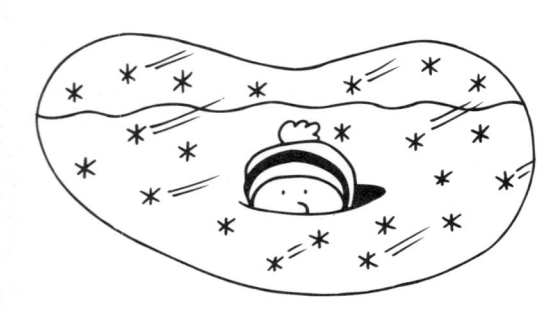

blizzard

Summer Success: Reading

Week 6

Name _____ Date _____

A Stormy Weather Story

Choose the kind of storm.
Write your own story.
Then draw a picture.

hurricane

blizzard

tornado

_____
_____
_____

Summer Success: Reading

Week 6

Name _____ Date _____

Word-Find Puzzle

Find the word sun four times.

```
R S U N T P
E G L S U N
S U N D B U
M N S U N F
```

90 Summer Success: Reading

Week 6

Name _____ Date _____

Rain Words

Say the picture name.

Add the word rain in each space.

1. _____ coat

2. _____ drop

3. _____ bow

4. _____ fall

Summer Success: Reading

Week 6

Name _____ Date _____

Self-Evaluation

1 Two words I learned this week are
_____
_____

2 Two kinds of weather I read about are
_____
_____

3 The best story I read this week was _____
_____
_____

4 This coming school year I will try to _____
_____
_____

Fold along gray line.

Take It Home!

Lynn and the Weather

Lynn likes all kinds of weather.

What kind of weather do you like?

8

1

Lynn likes a cloudy day.

Lynn likes a rainy day.

6

3

Summer Success: Reading 93

Fold along gray line.

Lynn likes a sunny day.

Lynn likes a foggy day.

2

7

Cut along dashed lines.

Lynn likes a snowy day.

Lynn likes a windy day.

4

5

94 Summer Success: Reading

© Great Source. Permission is granted to copy this page.

Week 6 Newsletter

This week we read about the weather. We read the book called *Thunder Cake* and a magazine called *Weather*. We also read two weather poems and a nonfiction story about a hurricane, a tornado, and a blizzard. Ask your child what he or she learned from reading and thinking about these stories.

The word of the week was *snow*. Children played word games using this word. They also made words from the letters in *snow* and completed word-find puzzles with *snow*.

Here is what your child has to say, in words and in pictures, about the week:

_____
_____
_____

Summer Success: Reading

Week 6 Newsletter

You and Your Child

One of the best things you can do with your child is to read! Set aside time each day to read together with your child. Many people find that a story or two (or three!) at bedtime serves as a regular routine to wind down the day.

Any books will do, but here are some titles that you might find at the library or bookstore. The books listed below are all about weather.

***Cloudy Day, Sunny Day* by Donald Crews (Harcourt Brace, 1999)** Cloudy days and sunny days are good for different kinds of activities.

***Hurricane City* by Sarah Weeks (HarperCollins, 1993)** A family uses humorous two-line rhymes to tell about the many hurricanes that have hit their city. There have been so many, in fact, that there is a hurricane for every letter of the alphabet, from Alvin to Zack.

***Rain* by Robert Kalan (Morrow, 1991)** Bold graphics of blue sky, white clouds, rain, and a rainbow are simply labeled.

***Rain* by Manya Stojic (Crown, 2000)** Animals of the African savanna use their senses to predict and then enjoy the rain.

***Snowballs* by Lois Ehlert (Harcourt Brace, 1996)** A group of children create and describe a family made of snow. A section at the back gives factual information about snow.

***The Snowy Day* by Ezra Jack Keats (Viking, 1996)** This classic Caldecott winner is about a little boy in a city on a very snowy day.